31 DAYS FOR
ADVENT
FOR SMALL GROUP
OR PERSONAL USE

My
beloved
Son

CWR

Michael Baughen

Contents

Introduction

'This is my beloved Son ... listen to him' (Matt. 17:5, ESV).

In this study guide we will delve into the wonderful Christ-centred letter to the Hebrews; a letter that is relevant in our time when many are only ready to think of Jesus as a good man rather than the Son of God. It was primarily addressing Christians who had converted from Judaism but whose thoughts were so embedded in the great writings of the Old Testament that they were having difficulty accepting the uniqueness of Jesus. They were unsure of His being God and thus superior in person and authority to all who had gone before. They also seem to be questioning the atonement and eternal life.

In the first of the four sessions in this study guide, we will look at the magnificent opening chapter of Hebrews, which is like a glorious overture about the Son of God. It may be especially familiar as it is read in many churches at Christmas, together with the prologue of John's Gospel.

In our second session, we will study passages from Hebrews chapters two to six, about God's Word being vital for spiritual life. We will see how our Lord Jesus, having shared our humanity, is so equipped to help us in our spiritual pilgrimage. Together, the Word and the Lord give us the firm and secure hope that anchors our soul.

In our third session, we will explore how the writer to the Hebrews draws on Old Testament scriptures to point to the wonderful truth that Jesus is our High Priest and Saviour. Christ Himself was the offered sacrifice for our sins. These readings will encourage us to enter into the benefits of salvation – most significantly, being able to enter into God's holy presence.

Finally, we will look at our pilgrimage en route to glory. Our fourth session covers the final chapters of Hebrews, which are about looking to Jesus and 'running the race' with courage and love, and not losing heart.

Some years ago I had the privilege of expounding the whole letter in four morning Bible studies to a huge gathering of Christians. After the third study, which concentrated on the great passages about the Lord as High Priest and sacrificial offering, and how this has resulted in opening the door of salvation, something quite unexpected happened. The whole gathering exploded into applause that was clearly not for me but for the Lord Jesus. It was spontaneous worship, praise and thanksgiving. As you explore the book of Hebrews, whether during Advent or other time in the year, I hope and pray that the Holy Spirit will light up these studies for you that you too may respond in heartfelt thanksgiving and praise to our Saviour and Lord, and be stimulated afresh to run 'the race that is set before us, looking to Jesus' (Heb. 12:1–2, ESV).

How to use this book

This book is designed to be read day by day alongside the Bible. As there are thirty-one days, you may choose to read it in the month of December, but it has been left undated to allow for flexible use. Each day begins with an opening prayer to focus in on the day's topic and to ask God for help to see His Word in a new light. This is followed by one or two Bible readings and notes reflecting on the scriptures. Each day also includes a suggested further reading to ponder, an idea for a time of worship (hymn lyrics can be found for free on the internet) and finally, a question to consider, which encourages us to apply the study to our own lives.

If you are using this book in a small group, all members will need an individual copy to read throughout the week. Then, as you complete each session, you can use the group studies at the back of the book to discuss and consolidate what has been studied in that session.

This is the Son of God

Hebrews 1

DAY 1

Son of God

Opening Prayer

Father, please help me in these studies to see my Lord Jesus in fuller light and to respond with a fuller Christian life, to Your glory. Amen.

Bible Reading

Hebrews 1:1–2

As my American friends would say – this is 'awesome'!

That God, who made this amazing universe, who brought life to this planet, has actually spoken to us, is awesome. That He has spoken through creation is awesome: 'For since the creation of the world God's invisible qualities – his eternal power and divine nature – have been clearly seen' (Rom. 1:20). But more so that He has spoken by word of revelation to prophets, poets, visionaries and faithful scribes, so that we could know His mind, His will and His love. Yet they knew there was something better ahead in God's purposes. They were right. Eventually God spoke to us through His Son. Awesome!

Years ago, my wife and I went to see the initial production of *Godspell*. The start still lives vividly in my memory. People came on stage one by one, dressed in grey cloth, with a sign round their neck bearing the name of someone famous in history (eg Confucius, Plato). When twelve of them were in line across the stage they all talked together (the programme note called it the 'Tower of Babble'). Then suddenly they split to the side of the stage in silence and there alone was the person representing Jesus. It effectively said, 'you name the greatest people and minds in history and none of them can hold a candle to Jesus Christ'. God has spoken through His Son.

Here in Hebrews, the writer values the prophets and others to whom God spoke, but now they move to the side of the stage – the true, full and final revelation of God speaking to humans has arrived. Everything in the Old Testament progresses *towards Christ's advent*; everything in the New Testament is progressing *from Christ's advent*. There will be no new revelations other than those of the rest of the New Testament in which the Holy Spirit led the apostles into a fuller understanding of the truth of God.

At the transfiguration in Matthew 17, the three disciples see our Lord talking with Moses and Elijah, representing the Law and the prophets, but when Peter wants to put up three shelters for them, the voice from heaven points to Jesus: 'This is my Son, whom I love; with him I am well pleased. Listen to him!' (Matt. 17:5).

God has spoken through His Son – wow! That very statement should fill our hearts with wonder. How greatly we should value, love, ponder, read and meditate upon Christ's words and His revelation by the Holy Spirit to the apostles – for His words are the most authoritative and important words ever spoken in all world history.

So let's listen to Him and let's continue to have the Holy Spirit illuminating, interpreting and making the Word alive in our hearts forever.

Ponder
1 Peter 1:10–13

Worship
Read Psalm 19 aloud.

Questions to Consider
Are you an avid reader of the New Testament with a sense of awe and wonder that God has spoken finally through Jesus, and that He has spoken to *you*? Or have you slipped into casual familiarity?

DAY 2

Heir of all

Opening Prayer

Father, as I think on the huge significance of Jesus as heir of all, please increase my understanding, my vision and my assurance in Christ. Amen.

Bible Readings

Hebrews 1:2
Ephesians 1:9–10

Many people today have inadequate conceptions of God. J.B Phillips' book, *Your God is Too Small* exposes some of these false ideas of God – which we can all be susceptible to believing – in light of the true greatness of God. The recipients of this letter to the Hebrews also seemed to have a Christ who was too small. This opening chapter magnificently lifts them, and us, to see our Lord Jesus in His greatness. As Queen Lucy says in C.S. Lewis's *The Last Battle*: 'In our world, too, a Stable once had something inside it that was bigger than our whole world.'[1]

In today's reading we see Him 'appointed heir of all things' (Heb. 1:2). You cannot get greater than that! But why use the word 'heir'? We use this for someone inheriting title or possessions after a parent's death. But God the Father is not going to die. The answer is found in the Trinity – the unity of the Father, Son and Holy Spirit and the diversity of functions and responsibility. We have just been shown the Son of God, and now we are told the area of His responsibility (the universe!), which is described as heirship in the divine purposes. And He was 'appointed', which means a definite action. Christ is seated at the right hand of the Father in the heavenly places 'far above all rule and authority, power and dominion, and every name that is invoked, not only in the present age but also in the one to come. And God placed all things under his feet and appointed him to be the head over everything for the church, which is his body, the fullness of him who fills everything in every way' (Eph. 1:21–23). And His 'inheritance'?

'You are my son ... I will make the nations your inheritance, and the ends of the earth your possession' (Psa. 2:7–8). Christ is truly above all. Any authorities or powers that threaten His Church are no match.

Christ being 'heir' has wonderful ramifications for us. In Romans 8:16–17 we read, 'The Spirit himself testifies with our spirit that we are God's children. Now if we are children, then we are heirs – *heirs of God and co-heirs with Christ*' (added emphasis). Our hearts should leap. Co-heirs with Christ! So many people pile up huge wealth but die taking nothing with them. Their heirs inherit. We die *and* inherit! And we have a great assurance of this promise. 'In his great mercy he has given us new birth into a living hope through the resurrection of Jesus Christ from the dead, and into an inheritance that can never perish, spoil or fade. This inheritance is kept in heaven for you' (1 Pet. 1:3–4).

As fellow-heirs with Christ, we will also inherit the glories of seeing Christ bring the universe together. We marvel at the discoveries in the universe now but these can only be a trailer of what will be an utterly amazing and thrilling privilege of watching heaven and earth brought together under His feet – heir of all things!

Ponder
1 Corinthians 15:24–28; Galatians 3:26–29; 4:4–7

Worship
Give thanks to Jesus, heir of all things, with awe and wonder at your joint-heirship.

Question to Consider
Do you live as one who knows that 'where your treasure is, there your heart will be also' (Matt. 6:21)?

[1]C.S. Lewis, *The Last Battle*, copyright © CS Lewis Pte Ltd 1959. Used by permission

DAY 3

The Creator

Opening Prayer

Lord Jesus, through whom the universe was formed, please open my mind to understand more of this wonderful truth. Amen.

Bible Readings

Hebrews 1:2

John 1:1–3

'Heir' looks forward; 'creator' looks backward. Both views are unequivocally about Christ as God. Those wanting to reduce Him to 'prophet', 'teacher' or 'good man' are trounced as He is shown to be *Creator* – 'Through him all things were made' (John 1:3).

How can we speak of both God the Father and Christ the Son creating? A simple human example may help. Person A has the creative idea for a big event and he asks Person B to take the idea, develop it and bring it to fruition. Both Persons A and B are creators. It is only their functions that are different.

The Bible starts with 'In the beginning God created the heavens and the earth' (Gen. 1:1), and God says 'Let *us* make mankind in *our* image, in *our* likeness' (Gen. 1:26, added emphasis). The Trinity creates together.

Paul's words are helpful here: 'there is but one God, the Father, *from* whom all things came and *for* whom we live; and there is but one Lord, Jesus Christ, *through* whom all things came and *through* whom we live' (1 Cor. 8:6, added emphasis). The Trinity is one; the functions different.

Another question arising from Jesus' identity as Creator is whether He was involved in creating every part of the universe. Some Jews believed that there are three worlds – upper (where God is), middle (air) and lower (earth). So the writer answers this question for them by saying Christ 'made the *worlds*' (plural in Greek; 'universe' in the NIV translation), which means everything above to everything below. Everything everywhere was created through Him (see Col. 1:16).

And what a creation! Day after day it seems we hear of new discoveries in the universe, in the human body and in our world. For the unbeliever these are just discoveries. For the believer every one of them is exciting, is 'thinking God's thoughts after Him' (Johann Kepler), the amazing and glorious hand of our God as Creator in Christ. And the reason we see discoveries like this is because our view of all creation is transformed when we are in Christ, because we are 'a new creation' (2 Cor. 5:17, ESV) and we see *His* creation with new eyes. We do not just admire a scenic view or the detailed beauty of a flower, or any of the wonders of the universe; we praise and worship the Creator because we know *who* created them. This is our Lord's creation.

The old hymn *Loved with Everlasting Love* has this lovely verse:

Heaven above is softer blue, earth around is sweeter green;
Something lives in every hue Christless eyes have never seen;
Birds with gladder songs o'erflow, flowers with deeper beauties shine,
Since I know, as now I know, I am His and He is mine.

George Wade Robinson (1838–1877).

Ponder
Colossians 1:15–20

Worship
Read aloud or sing the hymn above (you can find the whole hymn on the internet).

Question to Consider
How grateful are you for all the benefits of the Creator's gift of creativity to humans?

DAY 4

Son of glory

Opening Prayer

Lord, may the light of Your glory illuminate my mind and open my heart to deeper worship and faith. Amen.

Bible Readings

Hebrews 1:3
John 1:4–14

The word 'glory' appears more than 200 times in the Old Testament and to my surprise, more than 200 times in the New! It is used of the presence of God, it is used to praise God; it is used of the action of God. Always, it is about God. The Jewish rabbis created a special word for it, '*Shekinah* glory', meaning that glory was a manifestation of God's presence amongst humans. Now in Hebrews we read that the Son of God Himself is the glory and the presence: 'The Son is the radiance of God's glory'.

Some early translations used the word 'reflection' instead of 'radiance', but that misses the point. The moon, for instance, has no light of its own; it reflects the sun. But 'radiance' means the same light, direct from its source. The sunlight that dazzles us when shining into our eyes is identical with and part of the sun. We cannot look straight into it but we can look around at everything being illuminated by it. So we cannot directly gaze on the glory of God in this life but we can gaze, and gaze, on the glory of God in the human life of our Lord Jesus and view all life by His light. Thus John writes 'We have seen his glory' (John 1:14) and describes Jesus as the 'light of all mankind' (John 1:4). The Nicene Creed makes it crystal clear: Jesus is 'God from God, Light from Light, true God from true God, begotten, not made, of one Being with the Father'. Read this again, exchanging the word 'from' with the Greek meaning 'out of' and it becomes even clearer.

Wonder of wonders, this glory embraces us too: 'Christ in you, the hope of glory' (Col. 1:27). God wants us to know it and experience it. He said, 'Let light shine out of darkness' and He 'made his light shine in our hearts to give us the light of the knowledge of God's glory displayed in the face of Christ' (2 Cor. 4:6). So as we gaze on Christ, through Scripture, through meditation and prayer, we know and experience more of God's glory. Isn't it wonderful when that glory overwhelms us in worship, in seeing His creation; in the receiving of His love? It is a glory mediated to us in Christ. It anticipates the glory of heaven. Even more wonderful is the way in which, through the Spirit, 'we all, who with unveiled faces contemplate the Lord's glory, are being transformed into his image with ever-increasing glory' (2 Cor. 3:18). I expect you will know some Christians who seem to glow with God's glory, perhaps especially those in their senior years, particularly as they come to the end of their earthly life.

Let us pray that through Christ and the work of the Spirit we may, more truly, show forth the glory of God in *our* lives, or as Paul puts, 'we ... might be for the praise of his glory' (Eph. 1:12).

Ponder
2 Corinthians 3:16–18; 4:5–11

Worship
Give glory to God in heart, word or song. You may like to use the hymn *Love Divine, All Loves Excelling* by Charles Wesley (1707–1788), particularly the last verse, which fits today's reading perfectly.

Question to Consider
Look back a year. Has 2 Corinthians 3:18 been your experience?

DAY 5

The exact representation

Opening Prayer

Father, I am deeply thankful that You have made Yourself known to me through Your beloved Son. May I know You more today and throughout my life. Amen.

Bible Readings

Hebrews 1:3
John 14:5–13

At the age of sixteen I had a junior position in a London bank. Out of all the jobs I was asked to do, there was one that gave me a sense of importance, even power! In those days, money was sent in linen envelopes with a blue cross and they had to be sealed with sealing wax. This was one of my jobs. I would heat the wax, drop it on the back of the envelope and then would take the bank-stamping tool and, with all the force of a teenager, press it hard into the wax. And there was the exact imprint of the bank's sign in the wax.

Today, wax seals are far less common; you're more likely to see the use of a compression seal. Probate documents, for instance, have to have the compression seal – the exact imprint. A mere photocopy is not enough – there can be no chance of tampering or alterations.

The Greek word for an impression or representation is *charaktér* and it essentially means an engraving, as used, for instance, on a minted coin. Our own common use of the word 'character' follows this – the qualities that mark a person out. So here in Hebrews we understand the force of Jesus being 'the exact representation'. Not someone *like* God but someone with the exact detail of the Godhead, through and through. Jesus is not, as some of the recipients of this letter seemed to think, a lower divine being. He is exactly God.

'No one knows what God is like,' people often say. In the days of my involvement with Christian youth music and *Youth Praise*, I was asked to speak at a meeting of church organists. They were so against what we were doing. Then a 'modern' composer spoke. 'God is a mystery' he said, in a 'holy' voice. He then played some of his music. No one understood the music. He interpreted his 'belief' well!

But God *has* revealed the mystery. He has spoken and come amongst us through His Son. We *can* know what God is like! Jesus said, 'If you really know me, you will know my Father as well' (John 14:7). What is God like? We can answer: look at Jesus and you will see what God is like.

Through Jesus we will see God's love, His care, His teaching, His warnings. We will see Him caring for the sick, the blind, the marginalised and the poor. We will see His heart of encouragement and forgiveness, hear His promises and experience His Spirit. We can read the Gospels and know what God is like and how we can know Him personally.

Ponder
John 14:5–11

Worship
Give thanks for the incarnation and for the privilege of knowing God when we have come to Jesus.

Question to Consider
Are you always ready to witness to those who say 'we cannot know God'?

DAY 6

The sustaining Lord

Opening Prayer

Lord of all, please open my eyes to understand the huge significance of Your sustaining power as I praise You for the enormous comfort of this truth. Amen.

Bible Reading

Hebrews 1:3,10–12

In today's reading, we see that Jesus is 'sustaining all things' (v3). The word 'sustain' means 'to carry' – it is the word used when the four men lower their friend to Jesus through a hole in a roof (Mark 2). It is a word implying a sense of going forward. It is also used a lot in terms of bearing fruit and productivity.

The old Spiritual *He's Got the Whole World in His Hands* comes to mind! The Lord carries and sustains our universe. There is no place for the idea of God being like a watchmaker who makes the watch and then lets it run down on its own. He sustains everything and it is not by some great effort but 'by his powerful word' (v3). He is in command of everything.

It is said that early scientific advances happened because of belief in God as a Creator and also Sustainer of a stable universe. Scientific laws tell us about the universe, the forces holding things together, the effects of the moon, the planets and so on. But no scientific law can stop the earth going off its axis, or the balance of stars and planets going awry, or the earth ceasing to produce enough food. The only reason all things hold together is the Son of God who is sustaining it all. As Colossians 1:17 puts it: 'in him all things hold together'. From the beginning God made the promise that 'As long as the earth endures, seedtime and harvest, cold and heat, summer and winter, day and night will never cease' (Gen. 8:22). Only God could make such a promise!

At a time when there are fears of what may happen to the planet (such as global warming, violent weather changes, nuclear warfare and so much more) we may have confidence in Christ as sustaining everything, even though we should do all we can to prevent damage to His creation.

So what about the end? An important question in our Advent thinking. In Hebrews 1:10–12 we see the contrast between 'they' and 'you' is used three times. The time for the end is in the Lord's hands. Human hands may be involved in it as they were at the cross but God's will is sovereign as it was then. There is no chance of man destroying the world unless it is when God wills it. The Son will eventually 'roll up' the heavens and the earth like taking off a garment, rolling it up and casting it aside. In 2 Peter 3:10–13, that final moment is called 'the day of the Lord' and on that day: 'The heavens will disappear with a roar; the elements will be destroyed by fire, and the earth and everything done in it will be laid bare … But in keeping with his promise we are looking forward to a new heaven and a new earth, where righteousness dwells.' That is the supreme Advent hope!

Ponder
Revelation 21:1–4

Worship
Express adoration and trust in God's promises.

Question to Consider
In what ways can you act to help sustain the planet?

DAY 7

Whom angels worship

Opening Prayer

Lord Jesus, I join with the angels in heaven in worshipping You as my Saviour and Lord forever. Please open my eyes and heart afresh in this study today. Amen.

Bible Reading

Hebrews 1:3–14

It may seem strange that the atonement is almost slipped in to this chapter's great overture to the Son of God. But the book of Hebrews does what the books Matthew, Mark and Luke do. It focuses on *who* Jesus is before it focuses on *what* He came to do. The watershed in the Gospels is at Caesarea Philippi, where Jesus asks His disciples 'Who do you say I am?' (Mark 8:29). In Mark, for instance, Jesus *then* begins to teach them about the cross.

So here in Hebrews, the great exposition of the atonement comes in several chapters later. First, the writer is concentrating on who Jesus is. So, although the mention of Christ's saving act is a trailer of those later chapters, it is mainly to make the point that after it Jesus sat down at the right hand of the Majesty in heaven. Sitting down signifies completion of the sacrifice. At the right hand of Majesty signifies He is the Son, superior to all (v4).

The main overture ends here. But there is an additional coda with angels coming into the picture. This is probably because of those who were uncertain about Jesus as Son of God but were happy for Him to be some form of angelic being, something less than God (we still face this error today). So the writer brings together various scriptures, mainly from the book of Psalms, with which his readers would have been familiar. Then he quotes: 'Let all God's angels worship him' (v6). That should have settled it!

How do you feel about angels? Uncomfortable? Warm? Grateful? Once I preached about angels and the very mention of them switched the congregation off! But angels are a big part of God's kingdom. They were much thought of in our Lord's day. In this Advent season we will read about them during our Christmas services. They are mentioned more than fifty times in the Gospels and more than twenty in Acts. Jesus spoke of children having their angels in heaven (Matt. 18:10). And here in Hebrews they are part of the exciting picture of celebration.

You may have heard of or experienced the intervention of angels in everyday life. My wife was once adrift in a rubber dinghy, caught helplessly in a swirling current in a river estuary, when a figure appeared and silently pulled her to a safe position. When she looked back there was no one in sight, nor was there a single person on the extensive beach around her.

Angels are 'ministering spirits sent to serve those who will inherit salvation' (v14). That is their glad task. They must love doing it. And we should be thrilled that they are involved in caring for us (most of the time we will not even know!).

But let's finish with our eyes on the centre of the overture: the Son of God. Let's join the angels in worshipping Him.

Ponder
Revelation 5

Worship
Read or sing a Christ-centred hymn or worship song.

Question to Consider
Do you think angels have helped you in your Christian life?

Our Secure Hope

Hebrews 2-6

DAY 8

Listen to Him

Opening Prayer

Lord, please help me to pay close attention to Your Word and its warnings today. Amen.

Bible Readings

Hebrews 2:1–3
Matthew 3:17

Two boys were enjoying some time in their rowing boat, fishing, lying back in the sun and diving off for a swim. But they did not realise that they were drifting out to sea. They obviously had not intended to do so; they had been careless. Observers on the shore shouted to alert them to the danger. Could they be saved?

Here in Hebrews 2:1 we see the danger of drifting from the centrality of Christ and salvation. The drifting is not deliberate but through carelessness; it occurs not from rejection of the truth but from neglect, apathy and disregard. The only way to stop it is to turn back to Christ's word with 'careful attention', longing to know it fully and working to truly grasp and live it.

Apathy will try to justify itself. So the issue is one of authority.

During one Sunday service, where I was rector, a pneumatic drill started up outside the windows. It was impossible to continue with the service. I went outside and asked the man to stop. He couldn't do so, he said, as he had orders to drill. A policeman was standing nearby. I asked him if disturbing a worship service in this way was against the law. He agreed. The driller then said to the policeman: 'Are you ordering me to stop?'

'Yes' was the reply. The drilling stopped. It was a question of authority. And so it is in our passage today. Who has supreme authority? We saw yesterday that the recipients of the letter were quite taken up with angels. The belief that angels were involved in giving the Ten Commandments is borne out in Deuteronomy 33:2, Acts 7:38 and Galatians 3:19. But, as Hebrews 1 says, Jesus is superior to the angels. It was He who 'announced' salvation (2:3).

So what if we ignore 'what we have heard'? The writer to the Hebrews says that if we ignore our salvation 'every violation and disobedience' will receive 'its just punishment' (God's judgment is always just). Those who received this letter, from their knowledge of the Old Testament, would have known how God dealt with disobedience to His commandments and with abuse of His covenant love. Ignoring the great salvation through our Lord Jesus, the Son of God, will have greater consequences from which one cannot escape. The only way of escaping judgment is by turning to Jesus as Saviour.

At Christmas we read the angel's words to Joseph: 'he will save his people from their sins' (Matt. 1:21). The love of the cross is against the dark judgment of sin. We may not like to talk about God's judgment; we may even talk lightly of it to save a sense of discomfort, but let's not forget the dramatic significance of the word 'saved' and the magnitude of what we are being saved *from*.

Let us make sure we do not drift carelessly from the centrality of Jesus and the cross; let us rejoice in it with faith.

Ponder
John 3:16–21

Worship
Say or sing the hymn *Spirit of God, Unseen as the Wind* by Margaret Old.

Questions to Consider
Do you take God's Word as authoritative? If so, do you always seek to respond to it in thought or action?

The liberating Lord

Opening Prayer

Lord Jesus, I praise You for freeing me from the power of death and opening to me eternal life. Help me see this more clearly in this study today. Amen.

Bible Readings

Hebrews 2:14–15

1 Corinthians 15:20–26

On a visit on behalf of my diocese to one of the Solomon Islands, I was welcomed with pipes, dancing and singing. Then a wizened old man came over and said, 'When you go back to England, tell them we can never be thankful enough that they brought us Jesus Christ and set us free'. He then presented me with a ceremonial dagger, saying 'If they hadn't, we would have killed you with this'. It was a deeply moving moment. These islands had been cannibalistic before courageous Christians came with the gospel. They really knew what it meant to be freed by Christ.

In this Advent season, we approach the day when we rejoice in the birth of the Son of God. We will have various stimuli to praise – that He came into the world, that He came to die on the cross for us, and that He is now King of kings and Lord of all. Today's reading reminds us of another incredible reason why we praise Jesus. We were once 'held in slavery by [our] fear of death' (v15), then Jesus came and fought a once-and-for-all battle against Satan and He won; the devil's power of death was broken. Christ's incarnation as a human was *essential* to break (making ineffective) the power of the devil. He tasted 'death for everyone' (Heb. 2:9). He showed His power over death through His resurrection; 'it was impossible for death to keep its hold on him' (Acts 2:24).

When we are in Christ we are set free from the power of death. The sting is removed. Eternal life is gifted to us. We no longer need to fear death because it is not the end. When Myrtle and I came close to death in an aeroplane in Africa – due to a fault in the plane and the need to crash land – we found ourselves so held in love and peace that it was overwhelmingly wonderful.

We do not need to fear death, but still many people do. A friend of mine was working on a building site when, one morning, one of the men dropped dead. All, but the foreman and my friend, made themselves scarce. Then, as the two of them saw the dead man's wife approaching the site with his lunch, the foreman ran. Only my friend, the young Christian, stayed. Without Jesus, death is devastating.

There is something quite different to a Christian's funeral – yes, there is sadness at the loss of a loved one, but the service is also full of hope, joy, thanksgiving and praise. Thanks be to Him who broke the power of death and set us free!

Ponder
Read 1 Corinthians 15:44–58

Worship
Sing or say a worship song or hymn about the resurrection, such as *Thine Be the Glory* by Edmond Budry (1854–1932).

Questions to Consider
Are you at peace regarding your eternal destiny? Can you help others who do not have that peace?

DAY 10

The helping Lord

Opening Prayer

Lord, I face temptations day by day. Please help me today to see how I can better face them by Your grace. Amen.

Bible Readings

Hebrews 2:17–18
James 1:12–15

The first recorded temptation of human beings was the temptation to doubt God's word: 'Did God really say, "You must not eat from any tree in the garden"?' (Gen. 3:1). At the root of every temptation the devil throws at us is his desire to see us doubt and turn from God. The battle for the human soul continues in flagrant power today.

But we have been given great hope. Our Lord Jesus was 'fully human in every way' (Heb. 2:17), He had flesh and blood like us, the urges and desires of being human, and the influences and threats of the society of His day. He was 'tempted in every way, just as we are – *yet he did not sin*' (Heb. 4:15, emphasis added). Temptation is not sinful in itself, it is only if we fall into it. And it can be beaten! Here are three truths that will help us.

First: Jesus understands us. 'Both the one who makes people holy and those who are made holy are of the same family. So Jesus is not ashamed to call them brothers and sisters' (Heb. 2:11). Let that sink in! He calls us His sister, His brother. And we can call Him 'Brother' as well as Lord. Members of a family understand one another. He understands the power of the temptations we face.

Second: Jesus helps us. 'Because he himself suffered when he was tempted, he is able to help those who are being tempted' (Heb. 2:18). This invaluable help is freely on offer to us; all we need to do is ask.

As Jesus said to the disciples in the Garden of Gethsemane, let's 'Watch and pray so that you will not fall into temptation. The spirit is willing, but the flesh is weak' (Matt. 26:41). Jesus knew His own need to pray; He knew the weakness of the flesh. He sought and found grace from His Father. So must we.

Third: God always provides a way out. 'God is faithful; he will not let you be tempted beyond what you can bear. But when you are tempted, he will also provide a way out so that you can endure it' (1 Cor. 10:12–13). We need resolve to take that way out. It may involve physically removing ourselves from tempting situations (like Joseph in Gen. 39:12).

Thinking back to that first temptation and the attack against the truthfulness of God's word, we find a key weapon to overcoming temptation – putting God's word first trounces any temptation. When Satan tried to tempt Jesus in the wilderness, 'If you are the Son of God, tell these stones to become bread' (Matt. 4:3), Jesus does not just say 'No'. He restores the right priority. 'Man shall not live on bread alone, but on every word that comes from the mouth of God' (Matt. 4:4). When we are tempted with offers of gratification, wealth, status etc, let's prioritise God's will and His values in response. Let's turn from what tempts us and lift our minds to God and say with our Brother and Saviour: 'Worship the Lord your God, and serve him only' (Matt. 4:10). It needs resolve to do so. But Jesus will help us!

Ponder
Matthew 4:1–11

Worship
Say or sing the hymn *Jesus Calls Us, O'er the Tumult* by Cecil Frances Alexander (1818–1895), or say aloud the Lord's Prayer.

Questions to Consider
What temptations persist for you? Can you learn from Jesus how to tackle them?

29

DAY 11

Hear Him today

Opening Prayer

Thank You, Lord, that every new day is a new 'today' with You and Your Word. Amen.

Bible Readings

Hebrews 3:7–4:11
Matthew 3:17

If you are miserable then read Lamentations and you will become more miserable until suddenly, like a pyrotechnic display, these words burst out: 'his compassions never fail. They are *new* every morning' (Lam. 3:22–23, added emphasis). To start each day with worship and thanksgiving should be possible for even the most 'not a morning person' Christian.

In today's reading from Hebrews, the word 'today' is repeated five times. Here, the writer's pastoral concern is that the Word of God will be fresh each day and, more importantly, that we will respond to it while it is today. 'Let us ... make every effort' (4:11) and 'let us be careful' he writes as he spells out the dangers of turning away from God.

Psalm 1:1 details the stages of falling away: *walking* with the wicked, then *standing* in the way sinners take and then *sitting* in the company of mockers. You may have seen this happen to those around you. In most instances, this occurs when people have grown slack about God's Word – it is no longer *today's* word.

So our writer implores 'See to it' (3:12) for he recognises how subtle, how gradual the falling away from the living God can be. We need to 'see to it' that when we read our Bible and there is a call to action (something to do, something to look forward to or something to ponder) that we allow it to affect our thoughts and our actions.

What does *today's* word mean for you and demand of you in response?

If we find our daily Bible reading is becoming a burden or a bore, there is a very effective way of bringing it back to life. We can 'encourage one another daily' (3:13). For example, a couple of young people who travel to work together each day resolved to read the daily portion of Scripture (using the same system) before they would leave home and then discuss it en route. Great idea! My late wife, Myrtle, and I would use the same daily Bible reading notes and often share thoughts and responses later in the day. I know of older Christians who meet with new Christians to teach them how to draw on the Word each day. Encouragement in the Word lifts us and pushes us forward, keeping us on track in spiritual growth. Belonging to a Bible study group is a life-saver.

As previously mentioned, my diocese was linked to the Solomon Islands. Myrtle and I went there to establish the link. One afternoon, in the overwhelming heat, we sat in a simple chapel with a large number of young men in the Melanesian Brotherhood, all having given themselves to serve Christ. Their love of the Word was electric. They all listened to the readings and talk with rapt attention. For them the Word was for *today* every day. May it always be so for us too.

Ponder
Psalm 119:30–43

Worship
Read aloud Psalm 95

Question to Consider
The words 'disobeyed' and 'disobedience' are used three times in our passage from Hebrews. Are you aware of any areas of disobedience in your life?

DAY 12

The penetrating Word

Opening Prayer

Lord, please open Your Word to my heart and my heart to Your Word, now and every day. Amen.

Bible Readings

Hebrews 4:12–13
Matthew 24:35

In my twenties, when I 'woke up to God', one of the immediate evidences of knowing Him was the way the Bible became alive to me. Unlike any other book, the Bible is 'alive and active'. Once we start to read it, digest it and apply it we are never the same again. It changes us, changes lives, changes society.

Opponents of the gospel say it is 'brainwashing' that changes people into believers. How wrong they are. Genuine lasting faith goes to the depths by the Spirit, not just to the brain. As Paul writes: 'You show that you are a letter from Christ, the result of our ministry, written not with ink but with the Spirit of the living God, not on tablets of stone but on tablets of human hearts' (2 Cor. 3:3).

The Bible is 'Sharper than any double-edged sword, it penetrates ... soul and spirit, joints and marrow' (Heb. 4:12). This is vivid language – especially if you have been through an operation! But what do surgeons do? They penetrate through the body to get to the root of the problem – and there they get to work. That is exactly what the Word of God does. If we are open to the Word it will reach our inmost being, our sub-conscious motives, our hidden agendas, our deepest secrets – 'Nothing in all creation is hidden from God's sight. Everything is uncovered and laid bare' (Heb. 4:13).

The Word of God 'judges the thoughts and attitudes of the heart' (Heb. 4:12). The Greek word used here is used in wrestling, meaning 'taking someone by the throat'. That results in having to look the holder in the eye. The writer wants us to see that, when the Word convicts us of sin, we have to face our Lord if we want His forgiveness.

Now this needn't produce paranoia but rather a longing to be completely open to our Lord. Remember, He loves us beyond comprehension and He can be trusted. It is through this, sometimes uncomfortable, 'exposure' of 'the thoughts and attitudes of the heart' (Heb. 4:12) that we can seek God's forgiveness and changing grace, which make us right with Him again. So it can be uncomfortable, painful even, but it is worth the outcome!

Imagine if King David's sin against Bathsheba's husband was left unexposed. How far deeper he could have spiralled into sin. But God used the prophet Nathan to show David his mistake: 'You are the man!' (2 Sam. 12:7). God's word had penetrated and judged. David then faced God and repented very fully, as we read in Psalm 51. David's words, 'Create in me a pure heart, O God, and renew a steadfast spirit within me' (Psa. 51:10) can be our prayer too. May we be open to God every time we read, hear or preach His dynamic Word.

Ponder
Isaiah 55:6–13

Worship
Read aloud Psalm 139:1–18,23–24.

Question to Consider
What can we do to enable the Word to penetrate our hearts and minds when we read it and when we hear it read in church?

DAY 13

The sympathetic Lord

Opening Prayer

Lord, as I think on Your kindness and care for me, help me to be more caring for and understanding of others in Your name. Amen.

Bible Reading

Hebrews 4:14–16

We had experienced two miscarriages. Now a third was threatening. I walked into the hospital ward to be met by the Sister in charge with the words: 'It's gone.' Not a flicker of sensitivity, not a shade of sympathy; not a breath of love. Perhaps she regarded herself as one who should not be emotionally involved with patients. Perhaps she had never faced suffering in her own life. As the old proverb says: 'All sunshine makes a desert'. Little wonder I broke down and wept my heart out later that evening.

When the writer of our letter introduces the concept of Jesus as the supreme and final High Priest – the one offering the final sacrifice – there would be pictures in the minds of His Jewish readers. Earthly high priests would seem so remote, so apart, so holy, especially when once a year they went through the Temple curtain into the holy of holies. It would hardly be thought that they were sympathetic to the sufferings and weaknesses of the 'ordinary' people.

So, saying that Jesus, acting as the supreme High Priest and now 'ascended into heaven' (v14), was sympathetic to all believers, was and is staggeringly wonderful.

What do we mean by 'sympathy'? The Greek word means 'suffering with', not some easy statement of feeling sorry. We read that in the Church, as the Body of Christ, 'If one part suffers, every part suffers with it' (1 Cor. 12:26). That is true sympathy. And that is what our Lord, as head of the Body, feels too. He shares our suffering when parts of His Body suffer – be it in persecution, war, illness, homelessness or hunger. He knew hunger, tiredness, thirst, false justice, mockery, hatred; His suffering was expressed deeply in the Garden of Gethsemane and on the cross.

None of this would have been possible if He had not become man. So the wonder for us is that we do not believe in the false heathen gods – remote and imaginary – but in the incarnate Son of God, who shares the weaknesses and sufferings of humanity first hand. He understands.

It is because of this that we are encouraged to 'approach God's throne of grace with confidence, so that we may receive mercy and find grace to help us in our time of need' (v16). Thus, when Paul came to that throne with his 'thorn in the flesh', he was told: 'My grace is sufficient for you' (2 Cor. 12:9). Indeed it is.

Ponder
2 Corinthians 12:7–10

Worship
Sing or say Psalm 23 and give thanks to your caring, sympathising Lord.

Questions to Consider
Are you aware of someone who is suffering at the moment?
What can you say and do to express your sympathy, your 'suffering with' them?

DAY 14

Milk or meat?

Opening Prayer

Lord, please help me to keep growing in my knowledge of Your Word. Amen.

Bible Reading

Hebrews 5:11–6:3

'Will you help lead the boys' Bible class?' asked my vicar when I was demobbed from the Army. I hesitated. Every Sunday? I was persuaded. Three months on I came to crisis point. I had exhausted my knowledge of the faith. Though I believed, witnessed, enjoyed worship and fellowship, my faith was in the shallows. I would have been included in the writer's rebuke – enjoying milk, refusing meat.

Weaning babies off breast milk is challenging – they love the comfort. Sadly many Christians similarly enjoy the comfort of services, fellowship and the rest, but have not gone further to adult understanding of the faith. This is dangerous. The baby Christian 'is not acquainted with the teaching about righteousness' (v13). When they ought to be able to think and act like Christ in morality, in business ethics, in living by Christian principles, in having a Christian perspective on the issues of faith and happenings in society and the wider world, they are not confident or knowledgeable enough to do so.

Recently, a group of Christian students in a country plagued with corruption said they were shocked to realise that even in the light of such reality, they had a very shallow idea of biblical justice. So they resolved to immerse themselves into the Word of God, and they found transforming truths. They moved from milk to meat on those issues.

Verse 14 tells us that mature Christians 'have trained themselves'. The Greek word used here sounds like 'gymnasium'. So you get the sense of them becoming like athletes: devoted to and serious about their training. They can be *guided* by 'personal trainers' but the actual *effort* has to be theirs. The same is clearly true of any sport, any job or any pursuit. So training in Christian understanding should not be thought of as someone else's responsibility (vicars, pastors, small group leaders etc) – although they can help to guide us, we are in charge of our own understanding and maturity. And understanding is not an optional extra but a fundamental requirement in order to grow in Christian maturity. Put it first before any other training (see 1 Tim. 4:8). Don't neglect it or 'no longer *try* to understand' (5:11) as the recipients of this letter seem to have done.

And, wonderfully, when we 'move' on this we will 'be taken forward to maturity' (6:1). We move; God helps.

Ponder
2 Timothy 3:14–4:5

Worship
The second Sunday of Advent is known as Bible Sunday. Pray aloud this Bible Sunday prayer: 'Blessed Lord, who caused all holy Scriptures to be written for our learning: help us so to hear them, to read, mark, learn and inwardly digest them that, through patience, and the comfort of your holy word, we may embrace and for ever hold fast the hope of everlasting life, which you have given us in our Saviour Jesus Christ.'[1]

Question to Consider
Are you in training to be more use for God? If not, act today and say: 'God permitting, [I] will do so' (6:3).

[1]Extract from *The Book of Common Prayer*, the rights in which are vested in the Crown, are reproduced by permission of the Crown's patentee, Cambridge University Press

DAY 15

The soul's anchor

Opening Prayer

Lord, I thank You for the glorious hope You have given me. May my grasp of that hope become more secure and deep in this study today. Amen.

Bible Reading

Hebrews 6:13–20

I was once stopped by a senior politician who said: 'There is nothing left to hope for.' I sent an instant prayer to God, asking for the right words to say, and then replied: 'But in Christ there is everything to hope for.' He grunted and we spoke further. What he said is common among many people. They are 'foreigners to the covenants of the promise, without hope and without God in the world' (Eph. 2:12). They may talk in vague terms about heaven but they have no real faith, no real hope.

In Hebrews, there is much encouragement to hope. Back in chapter 3, we read that hope is set in Jesus as the Son of God, for He 'is faithful as the Son over God's house. And we are his house, if indeed we hold firmly to our confidence and the hope in which we glory' (v6). In today's reading we see that we can be certain of God's promises. As humans would swear an oath on some higher authority (eg 'I swear by Almighty God that I will tell the truth …') God swears (as there is nothing greater than Himself) by His very nature. He cannot lie. His promises are secure. Our hope is to be centred on God, on our Lord, because He does not change. He is the eternal security. There is no hope without Him. So let us eagerly take hold of this hope, or as the Greek translation goes, let's *seize* it.

In the Early Church there were three signs often used – a dove, a fish and an anchor. I believe we should restore the anchor symbol beyond hymnody. It is so precious to us when life is draining away or we are going through one of 'life's storms'. 'We have this hope as an anchor for the soul, firm and secure' (v19). A verse to write on our hearts! This anchor is buried deep into 'the inner sanctuary' (v19). Jesus is now High Priest for ever, in the eternal holy of holies. Our faith is in Him. He is 'our forerunner', who 'has entered on our behalf' (v20). Because He is there we know we will go there too, 'into an inheritance that can never perish, spoil or fade ... kept in heaven for you' (1 Pet. 1:3). So let's have faith, which 'is confidence in what we hope for and assurance about what we do not see' (Heb. 11:1).

Ponder
Romans 5:1–5; 8:18–25

Worship
Say or sing the song *There is a Hope* by Stuart Townend.

Questions to Consider
Look at Romans 15:13. How can we *overflow* in hope? How would you help someone who is hopeless?

Once and for All

Hebrews 7-11

DAY 16

Our High Priest

Opening Prayer

Lord Jesus, I believe You died for me; please deepen my understanding of this as I see You today as High Priest, forever. Amen.

Bible Reading

Hebrews 7:11–28

We may not readily think of Jesus as our High Priest, but to call Him such would mean a lot to the Jewish recipients of this letter, who were brought up with a system of priests and sacrifices – with the high priest as 'No. 1'. They knew that priests were set apart to function as mediators between people and God. On a day-to-day basis, priests would bring offerings and sacrifices to God on behalf of the worshipper, whether to worship God or atone for sins. But now the writer is telling them that priests are no longer needed, because Jesus completely fulfils this role. This would involve a great leap of faith for them, but it was a leap they had to take.

Some may have argued that Jesus could not be High Priest because He was not a Levite and only Levites could be priests. God had already sorted that argument out! Our writer shows that there is a superior line of priesthood in someone called Melchizedek, to whom Abraham gave tithes and who is mentioned in the Messianic Psalm 110: 'You are a priest for ever, in the order of Melchizedek' (v4).

Jesus is our High Priest who 'truly meets our need – one who is holy, blameless, pure, set apart from sinners, exalted above the heavens' (v26). We do not have to go to a temple or find a priest to get forgiveness; we can turn to our Lord at any time, in any place. The Old Testament high priest was a remote figure; Jesus as High Priest is closer than a brother. And unlike earthly priests, Jesus does not die. So 'because Jesus lives for ever, he has a permanent priesthood' (v24), 'permanent' being a legal word meaning 'non-transferable'. He could not, and need not, be replaced. Jesus is the final and eternal High Priest.

What does it mean that 'he is able to save completely' those who come to God through Him? Are we not saved when we turn to Him as our Saviour? Yes, as Ephesians 2:5 says, 'by grace you have been saved'. Let's use an illustration of a lifeboat to explain this: we are *saved* when we reach the boat, are *being saved* as we are taken ashore, and *will be saved* when we land. We are now 'in the boat' with Christ, heading for the heavenly shore. He is helping us grow towards Christian maturity, preparing us for the eternal harbour.

Today's reading offers us a wonderful encouragement: Jesus 'always lives to intercede for [us]' (v25). Jesus is interceding with the Father for our growth, interceding with care for us, love for us, longing for us. Similarly, in Romans 8:34, Paul writes: 'Christ Jesus … is at the right hand of God and is also interceding for us' and links this to the truth that nothing can separate us from the love of Christ. Our Saviour is praying for us! It is humbling and marvellous! And the Spirit intercedes for us too (see Rom. 8:26)! Our God cares for our spiritual growth and loves us all the way to heaven.

Ponder

Romans 5:1–11

Worship

Sing or say the song *In Christ Alone* by Keith Getty.

Question to Consider

Both hymns speak of Jesus as Priest and King. What do these titles mean to you?

DAY 17

Covenant of love

Opening Prayer

*Lord, I thank You that absolutely nothing can separate me from
Your covenant love – not now, not for the rest of my earthly life,
not ever. Please help me see more of the meaning of that love
today. Amen.*

Bible Reading

Hebrews 8:6–18

I get excited about covenant love. So some years ago I wrote a book
on it.[1] John Stott, writing the foreword, said: 'It is no exaggeration
to say that "grace" and "covenant" are two indispensable words in
a Christian's vocabulary, and that without an understanding of them
our Christianity is bound to be flawed.'

The old covenant had so much promise as it was established at
Sinai, with the Ten Commandments, the vows to obey God and the
shedding of blood to seal the covenant. God would be their God; they
His people. That the covenant was deep in the psyche is shown by the
various occasions in the Old Testament when celebrations, such as at
the dedication of the Temple (2 Chron. 7:3), were marked with the one
great song 'He is good; his [covenant] love endures for ever'. But as
Hebrews 8:9 shows, 'they did not remain faithful to [God's] covenant'.
Jerusalem fell; most of the people were exiled.

The way back would be through a *new* covenant. The promised
new covenant was announced through Jeremiah and repeated in
today's reading. Instead of it being nationalistic, it would be personal. It
is the love-filled covenant we know through Jesus and the Spirit – each
one of us able to know Him as Lord. It is for everybody. John exults:
'See what great love the Father has lavished on us, that we should be

called children of God!' (1 John 3:1). Jesus tells us: 'As the Father has loved me, so have I loved you. Now remain in my love' (John 15:9).

Here is forgiveness; sins remembered no more. In the old covenant, there is no forgiveness 'without the shedding of blood' (Heb. 9:22), which had to happen for each sin. But in the new covenant, forgiveness is made possible through the shed blood of Christ as the sacrifice for sins, once and for all.

So let us move to the Upper Room. The purpose of Christ's advent is about to happen on the cross. First, He gathers His disciples for the Last Supper with them. He institutes the simple signs of bread and wine, the symbols of His coming sacrifice. He breaks the bread and says: 'This is my body given for you' (Luke 22:19). But only when He takes the cup does He say 'This cup is the new *covenant* in my blood, which is poured out for you' (Luke 22:20, added emphasis). The establishing of the new covenant is with His blood.

So when we come to receive Holy Communion, we should seek not only to thank Him for our salvation but, as we take the wine, to rejoice in His covenant love and renew our side of that covenant with love and obedience. It is one of the most precious moments we can have with our Lord; we must not come casually, without thinking or preparation of the heart. It is a special moment of love. We are His covenant people.

Ponder
Romans 8:31–39

Worship
Say or sing the hymn *When I Survey the Wondrous Cross* by Isaac Watts (1674–1748).

Question to Consider
Look at 1 Corinthians 11:27–31. How could you better prepare yourself for the receiving of Communion?

[1]M. Baughen, *Grace People – Rooted in God's Covenant Love* (Milton Keynes: Authentic Media, 2006)

DAY 18

Our Saviour's sacrifice

Opening Prayer

I can never thank You enough, Lord Jesus, that You died for me. I ask You to deepen my understanding of Your enormous sacrifice. Amen.

Bible Reading

Hebrews 9:26–28

The angel said to Joseph: 'you are to give him the name Jesus, because he will save his people from their sins' (Matt. 1:21). To most people the words 'Jesus died for you' are meaningless. To so many, Jesus was just a good human, death happens to everyone, and the idea it could be relevant to 'me' today is ridiculous. Hebrews meets that challenge. Opening with the magnificent chapter on who Jesus is, it now shows us the depth of meaning in the cross and it goes on to show what this means for us.

Visual aids help most of us in learning, rather than just words. The sacrificial system was to show visually the seriousness of sin, the need to be forgiven and to be right with God. An animal taking the punishment one deserved was visually powerful when enacted by the priests. Anyone could understand it. I recall a young person, with minimal education, coming away to a Christian camp and hearing how the animal took what we deserved and how sinners placed their hand on the lamb to identify with it. I saw his face change. He understood the gospel.

In the book of Revelation, our Lord is referred to as the Lamb more than thirty times. When John the Baptist saw Jesus coming, he exclaimed, 'Look, the Lamb of God, who takes away the sin of the world' (John 1:29). When we speak of Jesus in Old Testament imagery as the Lamb of God we can better grasp the reality of His sacrifice for us, personally – 'you were redeemed … with the precious blood of Christ, a lamb without blemish or defect' (1 Pet. 1:18–20).

Sadly, there are some who denigrate the atonement and substitute it with a vague God-loves-everybody theme. They do not take sin and judgment seriously. God does. The Bible does. Hebrews does. We must. If we don't, then we can never have assurance of salvation.

Jesus 'entered the Most Holy Place *once for all* by his own blood, so obtaining eternal redemption' (Heb. 9:12, added emphasis). 'Christ was sacrificed *once* to take away the sins of many' (Heb. 9:28, added emphasis). We 'have been made holy through the sacrifice of the body of Jesus Christ *once for all*' (Heb. 10:10, added emphasis). On the cross, our Saviour cried out: 'It is finished!' If we look to that *once and for all* sacrifice, believe that He carried our sins and that we are cleansed as we put our faith in Him, we can have assurance of salvation. It rests on our Saviour's sacrifice, not on our deeds or works. Worthy is the Lamb!

Ponder
Revelation 5:6–14

Worship
Say or sing the song *The Power of the Cross* by Stuart Townend and Keith Getty.

Question to Consider
How might you help someone who has no assurance of salvation to find it?

DAY 19

Therefore draw near to God

Opening Prayer

Lord, forgive me when I come casually into Your presence and please show me more of what it means to come by the blood of Jesus. Amen.

Bible Reading

Hebrews 10:19–25

We can enter into God's presence. What a privilege! In human terms we would regard an invitation from the Queen to a garden party as a privilege, and it's a privilege usually given just once. But in eternal terms, an invitation from the King of kings to come by the blood of Jesus into His presence, at any time and in any place, is the greatest possible privilege for a human being, and is given forever.

In the Old Testament there was hesitation, fear, doubt even, about entering God's presence and so only the high priest could enter through the curtain into the holy of holies on the people's behalf, and only once a year.

Then, dramatically, the curtain of the Temple was torn in two from top to bottom as Jesus breathed His last breath (Matt. 27:50–51). The once and for all sacrifice had been accepted. No mediator was now necessary for people of faith to come near to God. People could boldly approach God with love and faith. And we are encouraged that, when we enter, the 'great priest over the house of God' (v21) is there, ready for us. We slip into His presence in worship and prayer.

The Jews being written to would have had to make huge strides of faith to see this and to act on it. We can all get attached to ceremonies; giving up irrelevant ones takes resolve. Here they (and we) are to come with a heart that really means business with God, not just putting up a front. We don't just need a bit of faith but 'the full assurance that faith brings' (v22). It involves thorough grasping of the truth and then a decisive step of declared faith. We are bidden to hold the faith 'unswervingly', knowing that 'he who promised is faithful' (v23) – what a lovely statement!

To enter God's presence we also need to have our 'hearts sprinkled' and 'bodies washed'. Perhaps this refers to baptism, but more likely, to ongoing cleansing. In John 13, Jesus distinguishes between having a bath and regular feet-washing. We need to regularly 'wash our feet', that is, consistently seeking forgiveness and cleansing, as we come to the holiest in worship and prayer.

We need also to be part of a living fellowship, meeting together at church and in small groups. Two things you cannot do alone – one is to marry; the other is to be a Christian.

It's clear from today's reading that some of the letter's recipients had become careless about meeting together to enter into God's presence. It is sad that, today, sports, leisure activities, family outings etc, weaken the commitment of many. Surely Christ should have *priority* each Sunday. I would like to take them to that country church on that Sunday night when an elderly man struggled up the snowy path. 'Should you be out on a night like this?' we asked, to which he replied: 'I would rather die on my way here than not come to worship my Lord.'

Ponder
Ephesians 2:4–13

Worship
Read aloud Psalm 84.

Question to Consider
When you approach God, how do you prepare yourself spiritually?

DAY 20

As the day approaches

Opening Prayer

Lord, please help me to grow in confidence as a Christian and to persevere in doing Your will to the end of my earthly life. Amen.

Bible Reading

Hebrews 10:25–39

'As you see the Day approaching' – the thought of the second Advent, or our death, sharpens the mind. When a Christian pop star was asked on TV: 'Supposing there is nothing after death', he replied, 'supposing there is'. The interviewer was speechless and his face went white!

In our reading today, the writer's heart is torn apart by the tragedy of people who 'have received the knowledge of the truth' (v26) and have not just fallen away because of apathy but have *deliberately* gone on sinning. They have turned into flagrant opponents of the faith, who have 'trampled the Son of God underfoot', 'treated as an unholy thing the blood of the covenant that sanctified them' and 'insulted the Spirit of grace' (v29). Trampling, insulting God – one's heart bleeds. It seems this is the blasphemy against the Holy Spirit that will not be forgiven (Matt. 12:31–32). We may ask, what made them become like this? Most likely they never had a personal relationship with God. It is a burden on my heart, and I trust yours, that we should do all we can to help 'outward only' Christians to move into that personal relationship and so be truly confirmed in their hearts by the Holy Spirit.

The thought of 'the Day approaching' is also a stimulus to Christian living. We see this in the parables of the foolish virgins, the bags of gold, and the sheep and the goats (all in Matt. 25). In Hebrews, the writer encourages the recipients of the letter on the way they have lived for Christ. They had suffered a lot, shared the sufferings of others, dared to stand with those being insulted or persecuted, and even put up with confiscation of their property. It was daring to suffer with those in prison because in taking food or clothing you were risking your own imprisonment. How did they do it? They knew they had 'better and lasting possessions' (v34). This altered their values from earthly materialism to eternal values of love and self-giving service.

The danger is that when we are persistently being attacked or feeling drained in our service of others, we can and do get tired. So how do we 'persevere' in doing the 'will of God' (v36)? Perhaps at least once a year (or as often as we like), we should take time with God to lay our lives afresh at His feet. These are moments when the offering of our 'bodies as a living sacrifice, holy and pleasing to God' (Rom. 12:1) can be renewed, as we seek to know His will for the next year, and pledge ourselves to do it. He will often open our eyes to fresh paths of service, or give us new strength for the same paths. Persevering should never be a chore or a bore when we have God!

Our writer ends with encouragement: those who 'do not throw away [their] confidence ... will be richly rewarded' (v35), and 'will receive what he has promised' (v36). Advent eyes look beyond the earthly to the heavenly – 'we do not belong to those who shrink back and are destroyed, but to those who have faith and are saved' (v39).

Ponder
1 Peter 1:3–9

Worship
Sing or say the hymn *Father, Hear the Prayer We Offer* by Love M. Willis (1824–1908).

Question to Consider
How can we help those in our fellowship who are finding it hard to persevere in the faith?

DAY 21

Longing for a better country – a heavenly one

Opening Prayer

Lord, may my faith be freshly invigorated as I study this next chapter and may my Advent hope be renewed. Amen.

Bible Reading

Hebrews 11:1–16

John Calvin wrote: 'Unless our faith be now and then raised up, it will lie prostrate; unless it be warmed, it will be frozen; unless it is roused, it will grow torpid.'[1] His words were prompted by Hebrews 11. For if ever a passage in the Bible can raise, warm and rouse our faith, it is here!

Faith is not something that comes and goes, it is something rooted and growing in us. Much like we cannot see the end of the line on a train but, once aboard, we know we're heading in the right direction. And the nearer we are to the destination, the stronger our assurance becomes. On the Christian journey, frequent reading of Scripture lifts our eyes to what lies ahead and so our conviction grows. We also grow in our personal relationship with our Lord, our Creator, and this gives us a divine perspective and brings assurance.

Here is the basis of our faith: 'anyone who comes to him must believe that he exists and that he rewards those who earnestly seek him' (v6). From this foundational belief, our faith may blossom in different ways. Abel showed faith by giving his best, from the heart. Enoch faithfully pleased God. Noah obeyed God, trusting His word, against all the faithlessness and mockery of those around him.

Then we have Abraham. When God called him, he 'obeyed and went, even though he did not know where he was going' (v8). The way God affirmed his obedience in going out into the unknown, leaving comfort and earthly security behind, must have orientated his mind to know that God would look after his *final* destination.

We experience foretastes of heaven. We have been given 'the Spirit as a deposit, guaranteeing what is to come' (2 Cor. 5:5). Yet here, *before* Christ came to earth, these people of faith had an inner awakening of heaven. Abraham was 'longing for a better country – a heavenly one' (v16), a 'city with foundations, whose architect and builder is God' (v10). Such faith is met by great assurance: 'Therefore God is not ashamed to be called their God, for he has prepared a city for them' (v16) – and us! No need to talk detail – that it is God's city is all we need to know. As a Christian we should always hold this glorious future in our minds and hearts. Isn't it just wonderful?

Ponder

Read 1 Thessalonians 4:13–18 and focus on Abraham in Hebrews 11:8–12.

Worship

Sing or say the hymn, *We Trust in You, Our Shield and Our Defender* by Edith G. Cherry (1872–1897) or *Come and See the Shining Hope That Christ's Apostle Saw* by Christopher Idle.

Question to Consider

Can you think of other occurrences in the life of Abraham that would have strengthened his faith?

[1]Calvin, J., *Commentaries on the Epistle of Paul the Apostle to the Hebrews* (Oregon: Wipf and Stock Publishers, 2007) p88

DAY 22

Looking ahead to His reward

Opening Prayer

Lord, help me to be inspired by the Advent hope, to choose what pleases You and to persevere in doing so. Amen.

Bible Reading

Hebrews 11:17–28

What a testing situation Abraham found himself in! He had 'embraced the promises' (v17) – he was a full-on believer. So how could God demand this sacrifice of an only son when this son was promised as the one through whom Abraham's 'offspring [would] be reckoned' (v18)? We are unlikely to have this sort of dilemma but we can, and do, face situations where there seem to be conflicting demands from God. The key here is in verse 19 – Abraham *reasoned*. He spent time pondering the situation. God must have a solution. It was God's problem! At no point did Abraham hold back from what was commanded. He was entirely open to God. His love for God was even greater than the enormous love for his son. God *would* provide the answer.

If we *decide* what is best and want God to *agree*, we will get nowhere. Very often my team and I (when I was a Diocesan Bishop) fell to our knees telling God we could not see a way through a serious problem. We rose and the answer emerged.

'By faith' we can trust God with our future, just as those in our reading did so wholeheartedly. Moses lived his life with an eternal perspective, and as such, He made a righteous choice that would seem extremely foolish from an earthly perspective. He had been wonderfully educated in Pharaoh's household and had a position of power in Egypt (Acts 7:22). But gradually he began to see what was happening to his people and eventually made the self-sacrificing decision 'to be ill-treated along with the people of God rather than to enjoy the fleeting pleasures of sin' (v25). When many young Christians find themselves battered by the world and its temptations, unsure of where true values lie in this materialistic society, this is a key verse of challenge. As is this: 'He regarded disgrace for the sake of Christ as of greater value than the treasures of Egypt' (v26).

Moses could perceive life this way because he 'was looking ahead to his reward' (v26). 'Looking ahead' means fixing one's eyes on one thing and deliberately turning away from the alternatives. And the word 'reward' here means something that will last and last – we now know that it is forever.

During 2014, a famous humanist visited Africa to see the refugee camps and centres of mercy. He wrote on his return that the only hope for Africa was with Christians because they persevered and did not give up on the task they were set. We persevere because we see God with eyes of faith. Like Moses, we can see 'him who is invisible' (v27) and trust our future is safe in His hands.

Ponder
Colossians 3:1–4; 2 Corinthians 4:16–18; 5:1–10

Worship
Sing or say the hymn *Jesus, the Joy of Loving Hearts* by Ray Palmer (1808–1887).

Question to Consider
How would you talk through verses 24–26 with a young or new Christian?

DAY 23

God had planned something better

Opening Prayer

Lord, may today's study strengthen me and stir within me the desire for greater prayer and care for my brothers and sisters who are suffering for Christ throughout the world. Amen.

Bible Reading

Hebrews 11:32–40

The list of heroes of faith continues in this passage with more achievements and triumphs. That is where many would like to leave the list. Churches and Christians that are triumphalist are loath to admit any defeat, problem, doubt or heartache, as if lacking faith. But the Bible is emphatic that suffering is part of the Christian life and that for many it brings terrible suffering for the faith (as it was for those mentioned in verses 35–38). No human success stories here, yet the faith shown in these verses is surely the greatest faith of all. Faith that will withstand any persecution or suffering has to be deeply grounded. It is vital that we deepen faith, hope and love in our lives when all is well so that we can stand when things are not.[1] Mohamad Fiaz was born into a Pakistani Muslim family. He was drawn to Christ by love. He still faces much opposition but says: 'When you know the truth and reality of who Christ is, you can't turn away from it. You'd have to be totally mad to turn away. I stand firm in that.'[2]

Back in 1949, as the Communists took power in China, 200 university students in Chengdu refused to accept atheism. They were indoctrinated for three months. Then in a public square they were asked one by one whether they would accept atheism.

The executioner stood alongside. The first girl said 'Sir, when I went for my three months' indoctrination I thought Jesus Christ was real. I thought the Bible was true. Now I *know* that Jesus is real. I *know* this book is true.' She was beheaded at once. All 200 students refused to recant and were beheaded.[3] Their faith stood the greatest of tests.

Those students knew their Lord, knew that resurrection lay ahead. Only the eternal perspective could inspire their courageous witness and martyrdom. In verse 35, those who were tortured 'refused to be released so that they might gain an even better resurrection'. They 'were all commended for their faith' (v39) and that faith was rewarded because 'God had planned something better' (v40).

We know that in the present day, to our horror, large numbers of our brothers and sisters in Christ face the choice of apostasy or death. We are unlikely to face such a choice but everyone has to face challenges to faith through illness, bereavement, disappointment and tragedy. It is here that a Christian, deepened in faith, is able to be a powerful witness to Christ. You may think of many like that. They have shone for Jesus, have had peace surrounding them, and have inspired others. They have the perspective of God's 'something better'. Do we?

Ponder
Matthew 5:10–12; Romans 8:35–39

Worship
Sing or say the hymn *Great is Thy Faithfulness* by Thomas O. Chisholm (1866–1960). Pray for persecuted Christians.

Question to Consider
Would your faith withstand the persecution many face today for being a Christian?

[1]Further reading: Baughen, M., *The One Big Question* (Farnham: CWR, 2010), particularly chapters 9–11
[2]Olofinjana, L., 'Counting the Cost of Following Christ', *IDEA*, January/February 2015, p25
[3]Aylward, G., Hunter, C., *Gladys Aylward: The Little Woman* (Chicago: Moody Press, 1982) pp133–134

Looking to Jesus

Hebrews 12–13

DAY 24

Fix your eyes on Jesus

Opening Prayer

Lord, please help me to keep looking to You as my Saviour, Lord and Guide, and to act whenever I realise that earthly things have taken priority. Amen.

Bible Reading

Hebrews 12:1–2

A visit to the barber, when I was a boy, involved having to sit on a plank that lay across the arms of the chair. The variety of bottles and instruments on the shelf always intrigued me. So I was frequently tipped under the chin by the barber's scissors with the words: 'Head up, head up!'

When we find the going tough as a Christian, we may need a clip under the chin to make us fix our eyes again on Jesus. Spiritual 'clips under the chin' may come by the Spirit, through the Word read or preached, by a friend's perception or a shock realisation of how we have strayed. If it happens, we must stop everything and take time to be alone with Jesus, to refocus our eyes on Him over everything else.

Today's reading reminds me of how my mother would always do a thorough spring-clean each year. Carpets, furniture – everything on the ground floor – was put in the garden. And when the cleaning was over and the furniture and ornaments returned, anything now surplus was removed. We all need a regular 'spiritual spring-clean' as believers to dispose of ways, habits and wrong interests that smear our witness or drag our spiritual life down. The writer here sees it as taking off unnecessary clothing and donning a basic running kit.

We are to run 'the race marked out for *us*' (v1, emphasis added). Let's take that in. It is tempting to think 'if only I was *that* person, or had *that* task, or was famous or did not have problems or illness', but we are to run the race set before *us*. So time and time again we need to be alone with our Lord and say: 'Am I on the right track? Are there things holding me back from Your will? Are there new directions You want me to follow?'

If we check our life choices, jobs, home life, moral values, use of our money and spare time then we can be more open to fulfilling the race set before us. Also, as we get back on track, we find the joy again of being in the centre of His will for our life – His 'good, pleasing and perfect will' that comes from 'not conform[ing] to the pattern of this world' but from the 'renewing' of our minds (Rom. 12:2).

Let's be encouraged to do this by the 'great cloud of witnesses' (v1). These are the people who have fought the fight of faith and gone on to glory. Character studies of God's great servants in the Bible, and in history, are such an inspiration. (We came across a few of them in Session Three.) Perhaps, like me, you find Christian biographies stimulating to faith, especially when they are honest about the difficulties faced as well as the successes in ministry. Our greatest example, however, and the One we now fix our eyes on, is Jesus – the 'pioneer and perfecter of faith' (v2).

Ponder
Philippians 2:12–16; 1 Corinthians 9:24–27

Worship
Sing or say the hymn *O Jesus, I Have Promised* by John Ernest Bode (1816–1874).

Question to Consider
What would/does a 'spiritual spring-clean' involve for you in the race you are called to run for Jesus?

DAY 25

Consider Jesus

Opening Prayer

Lord Jesus, I stand in awe at Your amazing humility in becoming a human being and dying on the cross for me. I pray I may model myself, more and more, to be like You – living for You with courage and grace. Amen.

Bible Reading

Hebrews 12:2–3

The high point of Advent is, of course, Christmas Day. Yet even as we celebrate our Lord's incarnation, we recall Joseph being told to call the baby 'Jesus, because he will save his people from their sins' (Matt. 1:21). Later we watch the Magi bring gifts that included myrrh, which was used as anointing for burial (Matt. 2:11) and we hear the aged Simeon tell Mary that the child will be 'a sign that will be spoken against' and that 'a sword will pierce [her] own soul too' (Luke 2:34–35). The shadow of the cross was over the manger.

Our passage today says, 'he endured the cross, scorning its shame' (v2). On my first visit to Israel there were two places that reduced me to weeping. The first was in the high priest's house, where you can see the cell where prisoners were kept during trials. There was no door, no window. It was a pit into which the prisoner was lowered like an animal. And Jesus, Son of God, was treated thus!

The second place was the pavement under the Sisters of Zion convent. Here are the marks of 'The Game of the King' or the 'King's Game', chiselled in the stone. This is thought to be the type of game being played when the soldiers mocked our Lord and put a cloak and a crown of thorns on Him and a sceptre in His hand – they played games with the Son of God. I still weep even as I write this. When we think through His life, especially when remembering the thirty-nine lashes and the crucifixion itself, we are left speechless.

The word 'consider', used in today's reading, is a mathematical word with the idea of reckoning up. It is an encouragement to all facing sufferings for Christ, to weigh up what He suffered and had to endure in His ministry and death. That He 'endured such opposition from sinners' rings true for our experience, be it mockery by fellow students or colleagues, being regarded as odd or foolish, being threatened even. It will not ease suffering but it will strengthen resolve to endure for His sake and His purpose, 'so that you will not grow weary and lose heart' (v3).

What does 'For the joy that was set before him' (v2) mean? It may sound like personal joy, but clearly our Lord did not aim for that. Rather, he set His eyes on the joy of fulfilling His Father's will – the harvest of souls that would follow, the great gathering of those who would find salvation through Him and His cross – that surely is the joy.

So for us, as we press on for Christ, even when we get a 'rough ride' from the world, the privilege of serving Him and seeking to do His will is both inspired by Christ's endurance and lifted by the joyful prospect of hearing God say to us, 'Well done, good and faithful servant!' (Matt. 25:21).

Ponder
Isaiah 53 (and see footnote to verse 11); Romans 8:18

Worship
Sing or say the hymn *Hark! The Herald Angels Sing* by Charles Wesley (1707–1788). Let us praise and adore our Saviour for coming to earth to save us.

Question to Consider
Opposition to the gospel is increasing. Are you ready to face it and respond to it with Christ's truth and grace, even if costly? Think of Jesus.

DAY 26

The Father's training of us as beloved children

Opening Prayer

Father, I want to be the best for You and I am thankful that You want that for me too. I pray that I may be open to Your loving correction and guidance. Amen.

Bible Reading

Hebrews 12:4–17

Do you have a personal trainer? If this question is referring to a physical fitness trainer, the answer for me at my age is 'No'! But if reference is to my spiritual fitness, the answer is 'Yes, God the Father'. And so it may be, or can be, for you.

'Discipline' sounds hard. It reminds me of my days in the Army or the times I was caned at school. Painful? Yes! But with God it is different; it is discipline, father to child. For the many who have suffered at the hands of their earthly fathers, this may invoke bitter or painful memories. So we need to focus on the fact that God the Father is perfect, and He disciplines the one He loves (v6) – yes, *loves*. It is not punitive.

It helps when we use the alternative translation of 'discipline' – 'training'. Any truly loving parent has a responsibility to train their children by guidance, correction, encouragement, example etc, but always with love. Petty restrictions or intemperate punishment have no place in loving training. God does not do that. The aim of our heavenly Father is to produce in us a 'harvest of righteousness and peace' (v11).

'Discipling' comes from the same root as 'discipline' in English. Jesus *trained* the Twelve in many ways. He trained them in faith and patience when His saving of them was delayed as they faced a dangerous storm. He trained them in seeking God for provision and the seemingly impossible when He challenged them to feed the five thousand. He trained them in using their words wisely, particularly Peter, who said both brilliant statements (declaring Jesus as the Son of God in Matt. 16:16) and foolish ones (causing Jesus to rebuke Him in Matt. 16:23), and in the space of just a few verses!

Sometimes we know when we are being gently slapped over the fingers. When, in my early twenties, I was called to ordained ministry, my choice of colleges at which I could train came down to one south of the Thames and one north of it. I could not decide. So I threw open the Bible and put my finger down. 'You shall take the north gate' it said. That settles it, I thought. Then I realised the college north of the Thames was at a place called Southgate. It was a slap with humour! I have never abused the Bible like that again!

Our Father also wants us to exercise self-discipline. We are to 'strengthen [our] feeble arms and weak knees' (v12). In other words, we are to train in praying and acting on what God calls us to, every day. It takes great effort! But the more we work on these aspects of our spiritual life, the stronger our 'spiritual muscles' will become!

What joy we have if our offspring grow up strong physically, morally and spiritually. How much more joy do we bring to our heavenly Father if we grow in righteousness and holiness as His 'true sons and daughters' (v8).

Ponder
John 15:1–17

Worship
Sing or say *Fight the Good Fight* by John S.B. Monsell (1811–1875).

Question to Consider
In what areas of your life, and how, has God personally trained you in the past?

DAY 27

A foretaste of glory

Opening Prayer

Lord, as Your Word shows me the glory of heaven – where I already belong and to which You are bringing me – so may my worship be deepened in thankfulness, reverence and awe. Amen.

Bible Reading

Hebrews 12:18–29

Imagine yourself climbing, or going by train, up a mountain. Every now and again you see the top; your anticipation grows. Then someone hands you a camera with pictures of your destination. You can't wait to get there! As we walk the Christian life we also get lovely glimpses of God's glory. Today's reading is like being given a divine slideshow of pictures taken of our heavenly destination – where, spiritually, we already belong. It is thrilling. We can't wait!

The writer, addressing the wavering Jewish Christians, first reminds them of the terrifying darkness (so frightening that Moses trembled with fear) at the giving of the old covenant (vv18–21). But then he wants them to grasp the contrasting joy and assurance of the new covenant family, of God being in the midst and of the eternal gathering of all believers.

From verse 22 on, we are lifted from earthly places to an amazing sight – 'the city of the living God' (v22)! (We recall Abraham looking forward to such a city in Hebrews 11:10.) Here we see 'thousands upon thousands of angels in joyful assembly' (v22). How impacting! We will surely join in, for the joy of being home at last will fill our hearts.

Then, there's more – we are told that our 'names are written in heaven' (v23) already. What an honour and what assurance! In Luke 10, Jesus tells seventy-two people to 'Go!' (v3) and witness to the many surrounding towns. On their return and in their excitement due to the successful impact of their mission, Jesus tells them that yes, they were given great authority, but there was something even greater to rejoice about – that their 'names are written in heaven' (v20). Though our witness may succeed and fail in life, this truth never alters.

Right at the centre of our picture of heaven, of course, is God, judge of all, and Jesus, mediator of a new covenant by His shed blood. All heaven centres on the Father and the Son, as should our earthly lives. We may be tempted to worship created things, but remember, these are all going to perish (v27). The kingdom received from Christ our Saviour 'cannot be shaken' (v28); it cannot perish.

The chapter ends with a necessary reminder that, as well as being our loving Father, God is still the awesome, all-powerful God (vv28–29). Therefore, when we come to worship Him, we cannot do so with casual, unengaged attitudes and hearts. He deserves much more than that. Yes, we can praise Him joyfully, but our worship should spring from our thankfulness, reverence and awe, for surely those will be the marks of worship in heaven.

Ponder
Revelation 5; 2 Peter 3:11–14

Worship
Sing or say the hymn *Then I Saw a New Heaven and Earth* by Christopher M. Idle.

Questions to Consider
In the light of verse 28, think about being in a service of corporate worship. How far do you truly worship? Do you prepare your soul for worship?

DAY 28

Love as God intended

Opening Prayer

Lord, I pray that as I continue my earthly pilgrimage to glory, I may live my daily life with ever-deepening love. Amen.

Bible Readings

Hebrews 13:1–6
1 John 4:16

We have just had our eyes opened wide to our glorious future but now our writer brings us back to earth. We still have a life to live for Christ *here*. Today's reading is about the greatest act we can offer this world. We can speak in tongues, prophesy, have great faith, give to the poor *but* if we 'do not have love' (1 Cor. 13:1–3) we are 'nothing'. We were created to love.

Here in Hebrews 13, we are told to *keep on* loving one another. Our Lord gave us the new commandment to 'love one another' *as he loves us* (John 13:34) – what a standard! In contrast to the world's vague concepts of love, God's love is self-giving, unswerving; totally faithful. If we love like God, Jesus said, 'By this everyone will know that you are my disciples' (John 13:35).

Today's reading highlights two significant areas in which we can love – communities and marriage. First, let's look at love in our communities. It is the most powerful witness to the world when we love those in our neighbourhoods, regardless of age, colour, ethnicity, upbringing etc. And the most negative witness when we don't. Sadly, some Christians seem only to focus on loving those at home or church, without thought for how that love ought to be touching the needs of the community, or the world. Perhaps because it is easier to love the 'lovely'. But unless our love overflows to all, it will become stagnant.

So we are to 'show hospitality to strangers' (v2) and 'remember those in prison' (v3), ie those whom others would avoid. Isn't this how Jesus loved while He lived on earth?

Another way in which we can love – and in doing so, witness – is through marriage. Marriage is to be honoured by all. Sexual relationships are to be kept pure because it is sacred. Amen! How society today has diluted this. It has become the social norm to divorce because you are no longer 'in love' with your partner; or to be unfaithful because your partner is not fulfilling their 'end of the deal' – not supplying all your needs. This is not love as God intended. It is far from God's perfect plan. What a witness we can have through marriage – marriage that reflects Jesus and His bride, the Church.

We cannot let our love be controlled by our feelings. Did Jesus *feel* like going to the cross to die for us? No! It was a self-sacrificing act, a choice – love in its purest form – the greatest act of love in all of history! Now we can love as God intended, because this love surrounds us and it will never forsake us (v5).

Ponder
Matthew 25:31–46

Worship
Sing or say the hymn *Love is His Word, Love is His Way* by Luke Connaughton (1917–1979).

Questions to Consider
Are you loving the 'unlovely'? What steps can you take to show God's love today?

DAY 29

God is pleased with such sacrifices

Opening Prayer

Lord Jesus, thank You that You gave Yourself up for me as a fragrant offering and sacrifice to God (Eph. 5:2). Please help me to live a life of sacrificial love and show me how I can more truly please You in this way. Amen.

Bible Reading

Hebrews 13:9–16

Tradition can be helpful but it can also be restrictive. Anyone brought up in a strict religion of 'do this and don't do that' teaching, can struggle to let go and embrace the liberty of following Christ. The Jews to whom this letter was written were finding it hard to let go of eating ceremonial foods (v9) and offering sacrifices. But these were no longer necessary as Christ, the sacrificial Lamb, fulfilled and finished – once and for all – the need for these sacrifices. Grace entered in.

The challenge then, to them and us, is: how are we to boldly make our stand as Christ's followers – what marks us out? Also, are we *prepared* to stand out and, if required, bear 'the disgrace he bore' (v13)? Today we read that we can make offerings and sacrifices of a different kind.

The first is the 'sacrifice of praise – the fruit of lips that openly profess his name' (v15), that is: spontaneously praising God for creation or beauty, for salvation, for His love. Do we *openly* profess His name throughout the day, and every day? No matter who's watching? Let's resolve to make this a daily 'sacrifice'.

The other offering is 'to do good and to share with others' (v16), particularly when it is sacrificial. The mark of sacrifice is that it *costs* us. Perhaps it costs us in time, energy, money etc. Our Lord made the point dramatically in Matthew 5:39–41: 'If anyone slaps you on the right cheek, turn to them the other cheek also. And if anyone wants to sue you and take your shirt, hand over your coat as well. If anyone forces you to go one mile, go with them two miles.' It is not something we do casually, nor should it be in effort to receive recognition and praise.

Finally, we can sacrifice in order to make a pledge to our Lord. I once received a phone call from an angry father: 'How dare you take £78 from my son. Give it back immediately.' The young man had decided to give his life to Christ. He drew out all his savings as a sacrificial pledge. He wanted it used in God's service. He went on to ordination.

All and any sacrifice we offer to God should be in response to the cross and our salvation. Let's 'offer [our] bodies as a living sacrifice, *holy and pleasing to God*' (Rom. 12:1, added emphasis). The turn of the year is a significant moment; perhaps it's an ideal time to renew the sacrifice of your life. Why not join me in doing so?

Ponder
1 Peter 2:4–10

Worship
Read aloud Psalm 103 or 148.

Questions to Consider
Is your *whole* life a 'living sacrifice' to God in thanksgiving for your salvation? What do you need to offer up?

DAY 30

Jesus Christ, the same yesterday, today and forever

Opening Prayer

Lord Jesus, head of the Church, may I grow in prayerful love and support for Your Church on earth and for all who minister in Your name. Amen.

Bible Reading

Hebrews 13:7–8,17–18

Jesus Christ is the same yesterday and today and forever. What a statement! No wonder it's one of the most well-known sentences in the whole letter. It is a reassuring declaration for the Jewish readers and for us. Jesus, High Priest forever, does not change; will not change. Christ who was born in Bethlehem is the same Christ present before the creation of the universe. Christ who taught the Word, performed miracles and gave Himself on the cross is the same Christ reigning now in heaven. The Christ we believe in will not change and so His word revealed to us stands forever.

Today's reading relates this to church ministry and leadership. 'Christ is the head of the church, his body, of which he is the Saviour' (Eph. 5:23). The Church on earth is responsible to Him for the progress of the gospel and the spreading of the Word of God. And Jesus cares and provides for the Church, just as we feed and care for our bodies (Eph. 5:29). Pause a moment and relate this to your own church or Christian assembly. Our Lord loves your church, and He longs for it to fulfil the mission He has given all of us.

Leaders have a huge responsibility and our writer wants us to think about them now. 'Remember your leaders' (v7). We are to think in detail about their way of life and to imitate their faith. Such leaders bless the Church and surely bring joy to the Lord of the Church. They will have taught the Church to look to Christ as leader and thus to bring major decisions and needs before Him in earnest prayer. These requirements are necessary if we are to have 'confidence' in leaders and 'submit to their authority' (v17). We should also be mindful of how their responsibility can be a heavy burden, especially as 'they keep watch over you as those who must give an account' (v17). The Greek word used here can mean sleeplessness and that would ring true of many in ministry who lie awake with spiritual concern for the people in their church. We are to make their work 'a joy' rather than 'a burden' with our loving support. Most of all they need prayer (v18). Prayer for their opening up of God's Word, prayer for the multiple pastoral decisions and actions, prayer for their own spiritual life to grow; prayer for their family.

Now, back to that amazing statement. I am inspired by it again as I write. It constrains my heart to be more Jesus centred, more Jesus uplifting, more Jesus loving, more Jesus praising. Do you feel like that? Is the greatest love of your life Jesus Christ, God's beloved Son?

Ponder
2 Corinthians 4:1–10

Worship
Sing or say the hymn *O Thou Who Camest From Above* by Charles Wesley (1707–1788).

Question to Consider
The statement 'Jesus Christ is the same yesterday and today and for ever' is used here in reference to the Church and its ministry. Where else in your life is this statement helpful, challenging or foundational?

DAY 31

May the God of peace bless you

Opening Prayer

Dear Father, I thank You for all You have shown me of Yourself and Your truth in these studies. I put myself under Your blessing of peace, with gratitude for all You have done for my redemption, and commitment to Your will for the rest of my life. Thank You for Jesus – Your beloved Son, my beloved Lord. Amen.

Bible Reading

Hebrews 13:20–21

Isn't it a lovely blessing? The recipients of the letter, as we know, had various queries and differences of opinion, but God wants them to share true *shalom* – a Hebrew word for peace referring to one's wellbeing, physically and spiritually, evoking a sense of wholeness. And our writer describes God here as the God of peace, breathing His peace over them.

Jesus wanted His disciples to know this peace: 'Peace I leave with you; my peace I give you. I do not give to you as the world gives. Do not let your hearts be troubled and do not be afraid' (John 14:27). Again, after the resurrection, He said, 'Peace be with you!' (John 20:19) when He came to the fearful disciples sitting behind locked doors. And then again He repeated the words as He commissioned them: 'Peace be with you! As the Father has sent me, I am sending you' (John 20:21). Imagine it, they were in great fear and yet were being told to go out as witnesses of God's peace! But that is precisely what He wants of us – faith so deep it yields action that is not troubled by what might happen.

When we face uncomfortable, scary or painful prospects, we must remember this. Getting worked up just doesn't help. Trusting God, and being filled with His peace, does! We hear many testimonies of people who have faced great struggles, such as battling cancer, who tell us that they have experienced a deep peace. Whatever happens day to day, God wants us to draw deeply on the reservoir of peace, which is within us as a fruit of the Spirit (Gal. 5:22).

The whole atmosphere of God's peace is evoked by calling Jesus 'the good shepherd'. His teaching in John 10 describes the security of the sheep – known by name and knowing His voice – even when thieves and robbers are around. He lays down His life so that the sheep can experience peace.

The latter part of the blessing prays that God will equip us for service and that He will work in us what is pleasing to Him, through Jesus Christ. So there should be an atmosphere of peace in Christian service, a deep peace underneath all the demands, a peace that others sense, a peace that pervades a Christian community and is sensed by the stranger. After all, we are the children of the God of peace.

Ponder
Philippians 4:4–9

Worship
Say or sing *Dear Lord and Father of Mankind* by John G. Whittier (1807–1892).

Questions to Consider
Have you experienced the peace that transcends understanding? Are there times when you lose this divine peace by worrying rather than praying?

Group Study Notes

On the following pages you will find suggestions for group study, for each of the four sessions of this book. The overall aim of these studies is to draw every person in your group closer to the beloved Son, Jesus Christ, by digging deeper into the Word of God.

Each group study includes a short recap of the entire session's daily notes, an opening Bible reading, six discussion starters and a final Bible reading to close the session. Each discussion starter indicates which day the question arises from, if you wish to refer back.

Please feel free to use the material in a way that suits your group, perhaps picking out certain questions for discussion or adding your own, and injecting times of quiet or worship where desired. Members of the group may wish to discuss something that came up in the session but is not covered in these discussion starters.

I hope you will find the lasting benefit of engaging with the whole letter to the Hebrews – a deeply rich and relevant book of the Bible!

SESSION ONE: THIS IS THE SON OF GOD

In this first session we have looked at one of the most magnificent chapters of the Bible about our Lord Jesus, God's beloved Son. We recognised Him as heir of all, as Creator who sustains all things, as the exact representation of the Father and the radiance of God's glory.

Read

Hebrews 1

Discuss

1. Imagine you are with a group of people and someone uses blasphemous words about Jesus. What would you do? (Day 1)
2. Christ is the executive of creation. For what in creation and creativity would you especially like to thank Him? (Day 3)
3. That we may have 'the light of the knowledge of God's glory displayed in the face of Christ' is spelt out in 2 Corinthians 4:6. What do you think this means? Is this a reality in the experience of any members of the group? (Day 4)
4. As Jesus is the exact representation of the Godhead, discuss some of the characteristics of God that we see in Jesus. (Day 5)
5. Share how you responded to the wonderful truth that Christ is sustaining the universe. Reflect on what this means for the universe and for who will end it. (Day 6)
6. Have members of the group had experiences that might be because of angelic help? Has this first chapter stimulated your interest in angels? They occur a lot in the Bible – can you think of some of those occasions? (Day 7)

End by reading Philippians 2:5–11, followed by praise and thanksgiving for and to our amazing Saviour and Lord, the beloved Son of God.

SESSION TWO: OUR SECURE HOPE

In this second session we have explored the importance of God's revealed Word, especially through Christ our Lord, and our need to take it seriously. We also looked at the chapters speaking of our Lord as High Priest – caring, helping, releasing us from fear of death and giving us hope as an anchor for the soul.

Read
Hebrews 3:7–13; 4:12–16; 5:11–6:3

Discuss
1. What do you say to those who dismiss the concept of judgment and thus see no need for salvation? (Day 8)
2. How can you help Christian A, who is 'in a state' about impending hospital tests and Christian B, who is confident of eternal life but afraid of the process of dying? (Day 9)
3. What are the main temptations facing us (and our young people) in today's world, and how can we face them and defeat them? (Day 10)
4. What have been your reactions to the writer's strong emphasis on hearing God's Word *today*? Do members of the group use daily Bible reading notes and do they help? (Day 11)
5. Our Lord's sympathy is true all the time, but have members of the group known particular touches of His love and sympathy? (Day 13)
6. How can we further mature spiritually? Could more time be devoted to Bible study or would attending a training course in a particular area of the Christian faith be beneficial? What has helped members in the group? (Day 14)

End by reading John 14:1–14.

SESSION THREE: ONCE AND FOR ALL

In this third session we looked at the rich passages about our Lord fulfilling the role of High Priest and of offering Himself once and for all as the final sacrifice. We've been encouraged to draw near to God and to have our eyes looking forward to all God has prepared for those who love Him.

Read
Hebrews 10:11–25

Discuss

1. How has thinking through the once and for all sacrifice by our Lord Jesus helped you? How would you try to help someone who feels they can never be forgiven for some action or incident in their lives? (Days 16 and 18)
2. What does the covenant love of God mean to you? Are you assured that His love is always with you even when you cannot feel it? (Day 17)
3. Have you been encouraged by someone recently? Share how they encouraged you and how this helped spur you on in your faith. (Day 19)
4. Share what has helped you to draw near to God (eg, personal or corporate worship, prayer, meditation). (Day 19)
5. Are you mindful of the second coming of Christ? How can/does it affect your Christian walk today? (Day 20)
6. Hebrews 11 lists great people of faith. Did this list encourage your faith? What occurrences in life have members of the group had that have also strengthened their faith? (Day 21)

End by reading Psalm 136 aloud together, adding the word 'covenant' before 'love endures for ever'. Members could contribute the first half of a verse with something they want to thank God for.

SESSION FOUR: LOOKING TO JESUS

In this final session we have been looking at the lovely chapters on following Jesus, of fixing our eyes on Him, of being prepared to stand up for Him and His truth against opposition. Also, we had a foretaste of glory, thought of sacrificial living, of church leadership and ended with a blessing.

Read
Hebrews 13:1–8

Discuss
1. What hindrances and sins do we find tend to distract us from keeping our eyes on Jesus? What steps could we take to avoid these? (Day 24)
2. Share experiences of God discipling you – whether directly, through the Word, through others, or through circumstances. (Day 26)
3. Consider and discuss the implications of worshipping God with reverence and awe. (Day 27)
4. How can we better love people as God intended in our communities and/or in our marriages? (Day 28)
5. How can we as church members give real love and support to our leaders? (Day 30)
6. Why do some of us seem unable to have the peace that God wants for us all? What can we do to help each other? (Day 31)

End by blessing one another with the words of Hebrews 13:20–21.

Why does a God of love allow bad things to happen to good people?

In this book, Michael Baughen's years of biblical study and life experience come together to address this 'One Big Question'. This book takes a comprehensive and very sensitive look at the whole issue of suffering, the 'why' of questioning the God of love and the 'how' of knowing Him and *how* to prepare for and handle suffering. Includes group and personal study questions.

The One Big Question

by Michael Baughen
978-1-85345-792-0

Seminars and events

Waverley Abbey College

Publishing and media

Conference facilities

Transforming lives

CWR's vision is to enable people to experience personal transformation through applying God's Word to their lives and relationships.

Our Bible-based training and resources help people around the world to:

- Grow in their walk with God
- Understand and apply Scripture to their lives
- Resource themselves and their church
- Develop pastoral care and counselling skills
- Train for leadership
- Strengthen relationships, marriage and family life and much more.

Our insightful writers provide daily Bible reading notes and other resources for all ages, and our experienced course designers and presenters have gained an international reputation for excellence and effectiveness.

CWR's Training and Conference Centres in Surrey and East Sussex, England, provide excellent facilities in idyllic settings – ideal for both learning and spiritual refreshment.

 CWR Applying God's Word
to everyday life and relationships

CWR, Waverley Abbey House,
Waverley Lane, Farnham,
Surrey GU9 8EP, UK

Telephone: **+44 (0)1252 784700**
Email: **info@cwr.org.uk**
Website: **www.cwr.org.uk**

Registered Charity No. 294387
Company Registration No. 1990308